CONTENTS

INTRODUCTION TO INDONESIA

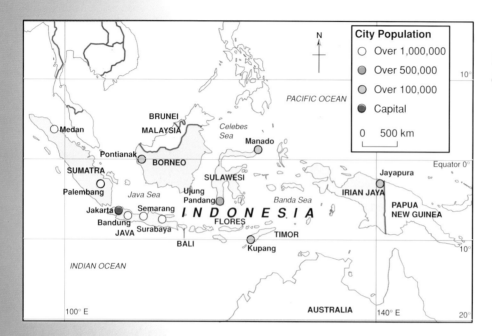

Indonesia: towns and population

Trade with the Indies

Indonesia is made up of 13,677 islands, though only about 3000 of them are **inhabited**. The **uninhabited** ones are too small or the land is too steep for people to live there. About 7600 islands are too small to have names. The Indonesian islands spread for 5000 km from east to west. This is one eighth of the distance around the earth's equator.

In 1492, Christopher Columbus sailed west to find a route to the Sulawesi Islands that are now part of Indonesia. The Sulawesi Islands used to be called the Spice Islands because of the nutmegs, cloves and other spices that grew there. Europeans wanted an easier way to get the spices than by travelling over land from the west. Columbus never got there, but he accidentally found himself in America instead.

Portugal took control of the area in the sixteenth century and made the area a **colony**. The Dutch took over in 1608, Britain ruled between 1811 and 1814, then the Dutch took over again. Indonesia was then called the Dutch East Indies. Local rulers often fought against the Europeans, but could not defeat them.

Indonesia

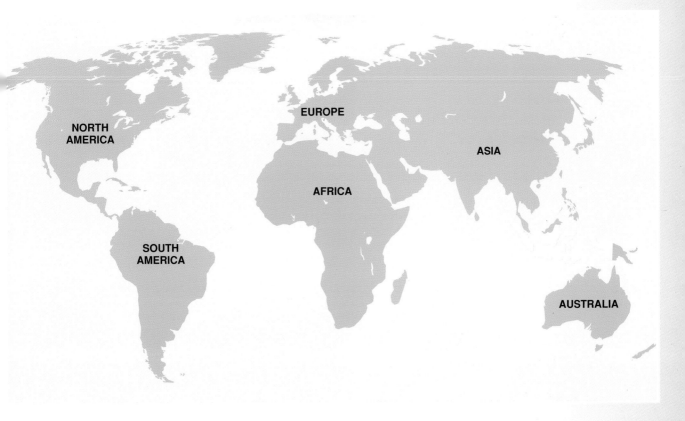

NORTH AMERICA

EUROPE

ASIA

AFRICA

SOUTH AMERICA

AUSTRALIA

Fred Martin

Heinemann LIBRARY

First published in Great Britain by Heinemann Library
Halley Court, Jordan Hill, Oxford OX2 8EJ
a division of Reed Educational and Professional Publishing Ltd

Heinemann is a registered trademark of Reed Educational and Professional Publishing Ltd

OXFORD FLORENCE PRAGUE MADRID ATHENS
MELBOURNE AUCKLAND KUALA LUMPUR SINGAPORE TOKYO
IBADAN NAIROBI KAMPALA JOHANNESBURG GABORONE
PORTSMOUTH NH (USA) CHICAGO MEXICO CITY SAO PAULO

Designed by AMR
Illustrations by Art Construction
Printed in Hong Kong / China

03 02 01 00 99
10 9 8 7 6 5 4 3 2 1

ISBN 0 431 01368 3

British Library Cataloguing in Publication Data

Martin, Fred, 1948-
Indonesia. – (Next Stop)
1. Indonesia – Geography – Juvenile literature
I.Title
915.9'8

This book is also available in hardback (ISBN 0 431 01367 5).

Acknowledgements
The Publishers would like to thank the following for permission to reproduce photographs:
Aspect Pictures, Fiona Nichols, p. 7 (top), Joanna Pegum, p. 14, Ronald Read, p. 28; Colorific Photo Library, François Guenet, p. 27, Ian Lloyd, p. 26; Panos Pictures, Jean-Léo Dugast, p. 11, Jeremy Hartley, p. 8, Chris Stowers, pp. 5 (bottom), 24; Robert Harding Picture Library, Paul Van Riel, p. 21; Still Pictures, Brecelj & Hodalic, p. 7 (bottom), Mark Edwards, pp. 19, 22, 23, Paul Harrison, p. 10, Dario Novellino, p. 15, Edward Parker, p. 20, Thomas Ranpach, pp. 25, 29, Hartmut Schwarzbach, p. 5 (top), Roland Seitre, p. 9; Trip Photo Library, pp.12,13,16,17
Tim Lester, p. 18.

Cover photographs: Zefa and Gareth Boden

Every effort has been made to contact holders of any material reproduced in this book. Any omissions will be rectified in subsequent printings if notice is given to the publisher.

A woman selling spices and other foods.
- *Food is often bought in markets like this one on Lombok island.*
- *Spices have been grown and traded from the islands of Indonesia for over 1000 years.*

The name Indonesia was first used in 1884. It may come from a local language where *Indos Nesos* meant 'the trading islands'.

Independent Indonesia

Indonesia was invaded by Japan during World War II. In 1945, people in Indonesia made a declaration of **independence.** They fought with their Dutch rulers until 1949 when the United Nations agreed to Indonesia's independence.

Irian Jaya became part of Indonesia in 1962. In 1975 when the Portuguese left East Timor on the island of Timor, it was invaded by the Indonesian army. Many people in East Timor want to be independent but the Indonesian government wants to stay in control.

'Unity in diversity'

Indonesia now has the world's fourth largest **population**. There are many different groups with their own customs and religions, and they speak about 250 different languages. Sometimes there are disagreements between the different people. There is a motto in Indonesia that says the country has 'unity in diversity'. It is often hard for them to live up to this motto.

In 1997, Indonesia's population reached 200 million for the first time. The 200 millionth person is a boy named Wahyu Nusantara Aji. The words mean 'divine', 'revelation', 'Indonesia' and 'precious'. On average, there are 8778 babies born in Indonesia every day.

Jakarta on the island of Java.
- *There are high-rise hotels, offices and other buildings in the centre.*
- *Jakarta is the country's biggest city and also its **capital city**.*

ISLANDS AND VOLCANOES

Country of islands

Indonesia is a country of islands. It includes a large part of Borneo that the Indonesians call Kalimantan. Borneo is the world's second largest island after Greenland. Two of Indonesia's other big islands are Java and Sumatra. Many of the smaller islands are surrounded by **coral reefs**. These reefs protect the sandy beaches from the strong waves that are whipped up by cyclones.

Some of the world's deepest ocean **trenches** are between the islands. The Java Deep Trench is 7727 metres deep. Narrow stretches of sea between the islands are called **straits**. There are many groups of islands like the Sulawesi islands. These are called **archipelagos**.

Dangerous places

The islands are mostly mountainous with steep slopes and narrow valleys. Small areas of flat lowland are usually found near the coast where rivers flow out to the seas.

There are at least 300 volcanoes in Indonesia. About 150 of them are still **active** and very dangerous. Two of the world's biggest volcanic eruptions were in 1815 when Tambora erupted, then in 1883 when Krakatoa blew itself apart. These eruptions killed tens of thousands of people. Many were drowned by giant waves called **tsunamis**. These are caused when the sea bed shakes during either a volcanic eruption or an earthquake. Many more people died from starvation after the eruptions because their farmland was ruined.

Indonesia: natural features

Steep slopes and volcanic peaks on the island of Bali.
- *The slopes have been cut into **terraces** to give more land for growing rice.*
- *Many of the volcanoes are still active.*

Dust, ash and gas

Some volcanoes, such as Mount Merapi on Java, constantly pour out clouds of steam and gases including foul-smelling sulphur gas. They erupt violently with little or no warning.

The Kelut volcano erupted in 1990 throwing lumps of molten lava as far as 35 km from the volcano. Roofs of buildings collapsed under the weight of ash and dust. Water from crater lakes flowed down the slopes causing mudflows called **lahars**. These smashed down houses and covered farmland. Tourists often come to visit lakes in volcanic craters. Lake Toba on Sumatra is one of the most attractive of these.

Indonesia's mountains, volcanoes and ocean trenches are caused by slabs of the earth's crust, called **plates**, that are moving towards each other. They will keep on moving, causing more eruptions and earthquakes for millions of years into the future.

A film called *Krakatoa, east of Java* was made about the eruption of the Krakatoa volcano. Krakatoa is in the Java Strait which is to the west of Java. The film makers thought that 'east' sounded better than 'west' in the title!

Canoeing through the forest.
- *Heavy rainfall and steep slopes means there are many short and fast-flowing rivers.*
- *The brown colour shows that the river is carrying soil washed from the steep slopes.*
- *This river is flowing through a **mangrove forest** near the coast.*

7

CLIMATE AND HABITATS

Hot and wet

Indonesia's climate is mostly hot and often very wet. The average monthly temperature in Jakarta does not change much from 30 °C. This is because Indonesia is near the equator, where the sun climbs high overhead each day. The heat from the sun is therefore very strong.

The lowest temperatures are on the mountain tops where there can be snow, even though the equator passes through Indonesia.

The name of the Pegunungan Maoke mountain on Irian Jaya means 'snow mountain'. It is about 4600 metres high.

Heavy rain falls between December and March when **monsoon** winds blow over the islands. Jakarta gets about 1755 mm of rain each year, which means it is very wet. There is a hot and dry season between June and October.

Rain forests

About ten per cent of the world's **tropical rain forest** is in Indonesia. About 60 per cent of the country is still forested. The rain forest has the greatest variety of plants and wildlife in any type of natural environment. There are at least 40,000 species of flowering plants including about 5000 types of orchid.

Tropical rain forest on Sumatra.
- *Tall trees with a canopy of leaves at the top grow up towards the sunlight.*
- *There is dense undergrowth where light gets through to the forest floor.*

The Komodo Dragon on Komodo island.
- *This is the world's biggest lizard.*
- *It is now an endangered species.*

There are about 3000 types of trees, including palm trees. Most of the trees are tropical hardwoods, such as teak. There are **mangrove forests** along the coast. Trees in the mangrove forest grow with their roots in the sea water and mud.

Wildlife habitats

The rain forest provides a **habitat** for many types of tropical birds including cockatoos and birds of paradise. Some animals, such as the orang-utan, live most of their lives in the tree tops. There are also butterflies and many types of insect and snake.

Some animals are now rare and may become extinct – for example, there are only about 1000 small Sumatran rhinoceroses left. The Indonesian tiger was thought to be extinct until a report in March 1997 said that one had been seen.

The Komodo dragon is the world's largest lizard. It does not usually attack people, although it is safer not to disturb one. They grow up to four metres long and can run at up to 50 km per hour.

The world's biggest flower grows on Sumatra. It has a bloom that is one metre wide but it only opens for about a week. Its name is *Rafflesia Amoldi*, or the Fragile Fantasy Flower. It is also called the 'corpse flower' because it has a foul smell, like rotting meat!

COUNTRY AND CITY

Traditional village houses of the Toraja people on Sulawesi.
- *The houses are on three levels to show the underworld, the Earth and the spirit world above.*
- *The Toraja people believe that the gods come into the house through the north end of the roof.*
- *The most important building is the food barn.*
- *The buffalo is a useful animal for farming and is also a sign of wealth.*

Living in villages

About two out of every three people in Indonesia live in villages where they work in farming and fishing. Each village is a small community with only a few facilities. Some have a primary school, a mosque and a small shop for local needs. Many villagers move to the cities in search of jobs and a better future.

Some villages have become tourist resorts, where people make a living by working in hotels, making souvenirs and performing dances. Kuta is one of the tourists resorts on Bali.

Living in towns and cities

About one person in every three of Indonesia's **population** lives in a town or city. The biggest city is Jakarta, with a population of 8.3 million. The name means 'glorious victory' in honour of a local battle.

Many of the city's historic buildings were built by the Dutch, who used to call it Batavia. There are also old Portuguese and English buildings. One church built by the Portuguese in 1695 has been changed into a museum. The Istiqlal Mosque in Jakarta is one of the largest mosques in the world.

The city was named Jakarta again when the Japanese army invaded in 1942. Jakarta is now Indonesia's **capital city** where the government meets. All the country's most important museums, theatres, foreign embassies and other public buildings are also there.

Living in Jakarta

A few of the city's population are rich. They can afford to live in expensive houses and blocks of flats that often have security guards. The poorer people live in **shanty town** districts, called **kampungs**, that they have built themselves.

Many kampungs are on low-lying land that floods easily during the **monsoon** rains. Diseases spread quickly because there is no proper supply of clean water and there are no drains or sewers. Some improvements are slowly being made but the scale of the problem is getting worse.

There are many other towns and cities in Indonesia. The largest, Surabaya, Bandung and Semarang, all have populations of over one million people. These are where most of Indonesia's new industries are being built. There are also smaller market towns and centres for local **craft** industries.

The Dayak people on the island of Kalimantan (part of Borneo) traditionally live in a large group in one long, wooden house. It can measure about 150 metres long by 6 metres wide. About 250 people can live in the same building.

Very bad housing conditions in Jakarta.
- *People improve these houses over time.*
- *The small wood huts over the water are toilets.*
- *Diseases spread quickly through dirty water.*
- *The area is fenced off from better houses.*

THE HARTJE FAMILY

- *The Hartje family outside their home in Jakarta.*
- *Jennifer is wearing her school uniform.*

Meet the Hartje family

The Hartje family lives in Jakarta, the **capital city** of Indonesia. They live in their own house in the Pusat district. This is one of the better districts of the city. They can afford to live there because both parents have good jobs. Robert Hartje works for the government. He has a job in an office. Mrs Hartje teaches English in a school. Unlike many people in Jakarta, they have a regular income from their work.

There are two children in the family. The oldest is Jennifer. She is aged 11. The youngest is Joshua who is 3. In many Indonesian homes, people live with grandparents and sometimes also nieces, aunts and uncles.

Jennifer's school

During the day, Joshua stays with some family relatives who live nearby.

Jennifer goes to school. She goes there in a small three-wheel taxi called a *bajaj*. Some children go to school on a coach, in a taxi or walk. Jennifer's school is a private school. This means her parents have to pay a fee. The school is called the Kristen Kanaan School. Lessons start at 7.00 am and go on until 12.30 pm. After lessons, Jennifer and most of her friends stay on in school for games and other activities.

- *A local mosque in the Pusat district of Jakarta.*
- *Most people in Indonesia are Muslims.*

The school is the shape of a rectangle and is on several levels. There is an open courtyard in the middle. There are no games fields because the school is completely surrounded by houses and other buildings.

All the children wear school uniform. In class, they sit at desks either on their own or in pairs. The classrooms do not have much on the walls, except some pictures of important people. There are about 25 children in each class. Everyone listens carefully to their teacher.

- *Children in a classroom in Jennifer's school.*

Food and shopping

Mrs Hartje does most of the shopping in supermarkets. Some of these are in the centre of Pusat. There are also many smaller local shops and some street markets. She brings the food home in a *bajaj*. The family enjoy eating meals with meat and prawns that are hot with chillies and other spices. They eat rice with most of their main meals. Their favourite drink is tea that has been grown in Indonesia.

- *Mrs Hartje buying mangoes in a street market.*

- *A three-wheeled bajaj is one way to get shopping home from a supermarket.*
- *It is easier to travel in one of these than in a car because of all the traffic.*

FARMING AND FISHING

Farm produce

For just over half of the people in Indonesia, farming, fishing and working in forestry are their main way of life. Most of the farms are small and family-owned. The people grow crops including rice, maize, cassava, sweet potatoes, peanuts, soya beans, vegetables and tropical fruits such as pineapples.

Coconuts are grown for their milk and for the oil from the copra, which is the fleshy inside of the nut. Spices including cloves, nutmeg and chillies are grown. Chickens and pigs are reared for meat. Many farmers hunt for birds and other forest animals. Some also collect fruits that grow wild in the forests.

Farm work

Rice is grown in flat **paddy fields** in valley bottoms. These are flooded with water to make the crop grow. Some rice is grown on steep hillsides. The farmers do this by cutting narrow steps called **terraces** into the slopes. Crops grow well in the fertile soil that has formed from volcanic rocks. The high temperatures and heavy rainfall are also good for the crops.

Using oxen in a field on Java.
- *The main crop is rice.*
- *Most rice fields are flat and small.*

A village boy on the island of Sumatra.
- *The fish trap on his head is made from rattan and bamboo.*
- *His catch will help to give his family a better diet.*

A traditional way to farm is the 'slash and burn' method. First, a small area of forest is cut down. Then the leaves and branches are burnt to clear the land. Crops are grown for a few years. The plot is abandoned when the soil becomes exhausted. The forest grows again and the soil regains some of its fertility. There is a problem when crops are grown for too many years and the land is left uncovered for too long. This ruins the soil and it is easily washed away.

The biggest farms are called **estates**. These produce crops such as rubber, palm oil, tobacco and orchids to sell to other countries. Estates take up only one per cent of Indonesia's farmland.

Fishing for a living

There are at least 3000 different types of fish and other creatures in the seas surrounding Indonesia. They include species such as mackerel, manta ray, shark, shrimp, tuna and turtle. Most of the fishing is done by fishermen in small boats. Indonesia is one of the world's top countries for catching shrimp. Whales are hunted by fishermen from Lembata Island, who throw harpoons from rowing boats.

The government wants to cut down about one-fifth of Indonesia's forests and give the land to farmers. This is to stop them cutting and burning new plots every year.

15

A COUNTRY TOWN

The Totok family

Most people in Indonesia live in the country. The Totok family live in a country town called Bogor. This is about 60 km from Jakarta. They are wealthy compared to most people who live in the country. They live in a big house and enjoy a good standard of living.

Mr Totok has a good job working for the government. He often travels to Jakarta either by car or on the train. Mrs Totok does not go out to work.

She does some of her shopping in a supermarket in Bogor. The family eat out in local restaurants about 2 days each week.

- *The Totok family outside their house in Bogor.*
- *The family have their own car.*

- *Mr and Mrs Totok eating a meal at lunch time.*
- *There are no knives, forks or spoons.*
- *The family eat rice, pork, chicken, prawns and vegetables with dishes of spices and sauces.*

- *A modern supermarket in Bogor.*
- *This is where Mrs Totok does most of her shopping.*

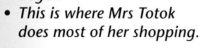

- *Aryo and Satria go to this school.*
- *Some lessons are held under the veranda.*

Going to school

There are two children in the family. Aryo is 12 years old and his brother Satria is 9. Both boys go to the same school. This is the Bina Insani School in Bogor. Most children who go to the school are Muslims. There are state schools in Indonesia where there are no fees. The Bina Insani School is a private school which does charge a fee. There can be up to 40 children in a state school. There are far fewer in a private school.

Classrooms in the Bina Insani School do not have walls or doors. The weather is so hot that it is cooler without them. Fans are used to keep the children cool. Some lessons are held outside under the shade of a veranda.

The school has far more space than schools in the cities. There are playing fields for sports such as football and rounders. Many boys are keen football players and fans. They can watch English premier league football matches on television every Saturday evening.

There are many different activities held in the school. Some children join the Scouts and Guides. There are also lessons in the **martial arts** of judo and karate.

- *These boys are learning karate at school.*
- *Karate is a way to defend yourself.*
- *The different coloured belts show how good a person is at karate.*

BUYING AND SELLING

A history of trade

Buying and selling has been a way of life in Indonesia for well over 1000 years. The Italian explorer Marco Polo visited Sumatra in 1292 because of the trade in spices. Spices and other raw materials are still exported. Now Indonesia's exports include many **consumer goods,** such as sports shoes, computer chips and clothes.

Country markets

Most country people do their everyday buying and selling in local markets. Farmers buy and sell small amounts of crops and some animals in village and small town markets. Goods, such as basketwork, mats, furniture and jewellery, are made by men and women in the villages. These **craft** skills are passed on through the family.

Some art and craft goods are now sold as souvenirs in tourist areas. Colourful batik clothes and ornaments carved from wood are special favourites with tourists.

City shopping

In Jakarta and the other main cities, there are department stores, supermarkets and modern high-tech shopping malls. The Blok M shopping mall in Jakarta is one of the most modern of these.

*A shopping mall in Jakarta, the **capital city**.*
- *Most of the wealthy people in Indonesia live in the cities.*
- *Shopping malls sell a wide range of expensive goods.*

A street market in Denpasar, the main city on Bali.
- *Farmers bring their produce to sell in the city markets.*
- *Denpasar is a city with a **population** of 300,000.*

The biggest and most specialized markets, such as the Sunda Kelapa fish market, are in the cities. Tropical song birds are sold in the bird market at Jalan Pramuka.

There are also street markets where consumer goods including clothes, watches and electrical goods are sold. Goods sometimes have expensive designer labels but they may be cheap copies that have been made illegally. The buyers and sellers usually bargain until a price is agreed. This can be as low as half the first asking price.

There are local street markets in every district. Food is sold from street stalls called *warungs*. Some of these stay open for 24 hours a day so as not to lose any business. Street pedlars are a common sight in the cities. Some make goods from **recycled** waste such as car tyres or scrap metal.

In Banjarmasin in Kalimantan, the market is held on small boats that pack together on the city's main river. Buyers step from boat to boat or paddle their own small boats to get about.

Batik patterns are made by painting hot wax onto the cloth with a bamboo stick called a *canting tulis*. The wax only allows colour dye to get to the cloth in some places. A more modern method is to use paintbrushes to apply the wax.

INDONESIAN COOKING

The basic diet

Indonesian cooking mainly uses foods from local farms and from local fishing ports. Rice, maize, cassava and sweet potatoes are **staple foods**. Most dishes are made with vegetables, including beans, shallots and cabbages. *Gado-gado* is a meal made from carrots, potatoes and hard-boiled eggs. It is usually served with a peanut and coconut milk sauce.

Hot and spicy

Many different spices are used in Indonesian cooking. Cloves, nutmeg, ginger and spices that make curry mixtures are often among the ingredients. *Trasi* is a spicy paste made from shrimps. Lemon juice and lime leaves are used to give extra flavour. One guide book takes care to warn tourists about small 'fiery red and green peppers'. A *sambal* is a spicy dip that is often served with meals. Some recipes have also been introduced to Indonesia from other Asian countries such as Thailand, China and Malaysia.

Preparing food.
- *Cooking a meal of rice over an open fire.*
- *Rice is the main meal for most people in Indonesia.*

20

A family eating out at a restaurant.
- There are many different kinds of vegetables and other foods served in small dishes.
- People eat with their fingers, with chopsticks and sometimes with a spoon.

Special dishes

Indonesian dishes are usually cooked in an open pan or in a large bowl-shaped container called a *wok*. Some dishes may include lamb, beef, chicken and pork. Roast suckling pig is a special dish from Bali. On many of the other islands, the people are Muslims and are not allowed to eat pork. There are also traditional fish dishes using shrimps, tuna and other local catches.

Sauces are made from coconut milk, peanuts and soya beans. *Saté* is a dish prepared with chunks of meat or fish, grilled on an open coal or charcoal fire, then dipped in peanut sauce. Soup called *soto ajam* is made from rice, vegetables and chicken.

Nasi Goreng is a common dish using rice, eggs and a mixture of vegetables and peppers. First, the rice is fried in oil in a pan, then it is mixed with egg to make an omelette. This is cut into strips and different types of vegetables and peppers are added. Chunks of meat or chicken can also be added and stir-fried until they are cooked. It is best to make this dish early in the morning, when the rice is still cold. If it is left until later in the day, when the temperature is higher and the rice is warm, it soaks up the cooking oil and it goes mushy.

Indonesians often eat while sitting on the floor. The food is put on plates and bowls on a tablecloth. They normally eat with the fingers of their right hands. This is a Muslim custom.

21

MADE IN INDONESIA

Rubber tapping.
- *Rubber trees were brought to Indonesia in the nineteenth century as a plantation crop.*
- *The rubber tapper makes a cut in the bark so that the natural rubber drips into a collecting pot.*
- *Natural rubber is called latex.*
- *The rubber is processed in factories.*

From clothes to computer chips

Thirty years ago, it was unusual to see the words 'Made in Indonesia' on goods. But Indonesia has a 'tiger' economy that is in a hurry to become rich. Now there is likely to be something made in Indonesia in most homes in rich countries, such as the UK and Australia. This may be anything from sports shoes and clothes to computer microchips.

Some of these goods are made by **multi-national companies**. Two of them are the Coca-Cola Corporation and the Goodyear Tyre and Rubber Co.

Natural resources

Some goods are produced from the country's natural resources. About four million people's jobs involve using wood from the forests. They may work in **logging** or in factories that make pulp, paper, plywood and furniture. Timber is also exported to other countries. About 1.7 million hectares of forest are cut down every year. A major problem is that few new trees are planted to replace them.

The Natuna **gasfield** is the world's largest known source of natural gas. There is enough oil to make Indonesia the fifteenth largest oil-producer in the world. Oil and natural gas supply energy for Indonesia's new factories. They also provide raw materials to make plastics, fertilizers and other chemicals. Metals such as tin, bauxite and copper are mined and mostly exported.

The new industries

Electronic goods including computers, videos and televisions are made in Indonesia. The Indonesian population of 200 million is almost as big as that of the European Union (EU) countries or the USA. However, these goods are too expensive for most Indonesians to buy, so they are exported and sold in richer countries instead.

The low wages paid to Indonesian workers, together with their skills and their willingness to work hard, have encouraged companies to open factories there and make big profits. Some multi-national companies have moved their production from countries where wages are higher. In March 1997, a UK newspaper claimed that toys and other products that are sold in the UK and the USA were being made by children in Indonesian factories. Children are paid even less than adults for the work. Young children often work in factories despite laws which try to prevent this.

Indonesia is called a Newly Industrialized Country (NIC) because it has so many new industries. It is trying to become as rich as other Asian countries such as South Korea and Japan.

Women at work in a textile mill in Indonesia.
- *Cloth is **mass-produced** using factory methods.*
- *Workers in Indonesia work for much lower wages than people in countries such as the UK or Japan.*

TRANSPORT

Travel by road.
- *Travel is often difficult away from the few main roads.*
- *Heavy rain and floods can wash away bridges and ruin the roads' surfaces.*

Stretching time

People who travel in Indonesia soon get used to the words *jam kare*. These words refer to something that stretches like rubber, and this is what seems to happen to time and travel timetables. Road conditions show why this can be a problem.

There are 219,000 km of roads in Indonesia though only 13,000 km of them are classed as main roads. There are only 200 km of motorway in the whole country. Steep slopes and heavy **monsoon** rains can badly affect the roads. Vehicles that break down are difficult to repair because spare parts are hard to get.

The lack of main roads and motorways is not a problem for most people. Not many people own cars and they only need to travel to their local market town. People use rural buses to travel to the towns.

City travel

The situation in Jakarta is different. Traffic congestion clogs the city streets. New roads and public transport services have not kept up with the city's rapid growth in **population** and the extra cars. People use double-decker buses, minivans and different types of tricycle to get about the city.

A pedal-powered tricycle taxi called a *betejak* or a motorized *heleak* can be the quickest way to travel. *Betejaks* are banned from the city centre of Jakarta.

Rail, air and sea

Most of the country's 7000 km of railway track is on the larger islands of Java, Sumatra and Madura. It is not worth building railway lines on the smaller islands where there are so few people. It is also difficult and expensive to build railway lines through mountains.

People travel between the islands by air or by ferry boat. Sometimes, there is a disaster when an overcrowded ferry boat runs into bad weather. There are about 300 ports but only about 20 of them can take ships over 500 tonnes.

Travel by river is difficult because most rivers flow too quickly and are too narrow and shallow for boats. The exception is on Kalimantan where the River Barito and its tributaries are **navigable**. There are river buses called *klotok* that local people use. Speedboats are hired by tourists who are in a hurry.

There is a cog railway on Java that runs for 50 km between the villages of Ambarawa and Bedono near Semarang. A cog system helps the train to grip the track on steep slopes.

Travel by boat.
- *Ferry boats sail between the islands taking goods, passengers and vehicles.*
- *Most harbours are only able to take small boats.*

ART, CRAFTS AND LEISURE

Local crafts

People in countryside areas of Indonesia often use their spare time to make goods they need or can sell. These are mostly **craft** objects made from local raw materials. The people make mats from coconut fibres and baskets from rice straw. Figures or tools and musical instruments are carved from wood.

Music, dance and sport

Music and dancing are important parts of Indonesian village life. On Java and Bali, *gamelan* orchestras use metal and wood gongs. The tune is played on bamboo flutes. The instruments in a gamelan orchestra are specially tuned to play with the other instruments in the same orchestra.

Slow and graceful dances telling stories about gods or ancient princes are performed to the music. Some performances go on all night. Shorter performances are put on just for tourists. Indonesia is also known for its puppet plays. The puppets, called marionettes, are large figures worked by strings.

Silat Gerak Pilihan is an Indonesian form of **martial arts**. As well as being a form of self-defence, it is a way to exercise the body and mind. To make the sport safe, blows are not allowed to the body or head. A stick called a *toya* and a machete called a *golol* are also used in the fighting.

Carvings in wood.
- *A village craftsman on Bali uses traditional skills to carve a figure.*
- *Many of these carvings are sold to tourists.*

Music and dancing on Java.

- *Many dances on Java are performed with masks.*
- *The gamelan orchestra accompanies the dancer with gongs, drums and wood instruments.*

Cities and tourist areas

The biggest towns and cities have parks, cinemas, restaurants and other forms of entertainment. Going to the cinema is a popular pastime in many Asian countries. There are 40 cinemas in Jakarta to choose from.

A new 9.5 hectare theme park, called Fantasy Land, has been opened in Jakarta. This is part of a larger leisure complex called the Jaya Ancol Dreamland, where there are facilities for swimming, fishing and other sports. The attractions of the park include daily shows of dolphins and sea lions in an aquarium.

For tourists, there are tropical beaches, mountain scenery with volcanoes and the chance to see a different culture. About four million tourists visit Indonesia every year and the number is rising.

Some visitors are called **ecotourists**. They come to see the wildlife and natural vegetation, but they make sure that they do not destroy it.

Badminton is one of the country's favourite sports. In 1997, an Indonesian called Heryanto Arbiis was world badminton champion.

CUSTOMS AND FESTIVALS

Religion and festivals

Many of Indonesia's customs and festivals are to do with people's religions. Although almost nine out of every ten Indonesians are Muslims, the people on Bali are mainly Hindus. There are a few Indonesian Christians. Some people worship natural spirits, especially in the more remote islands. Local people have often combined the beliefs and festivals of different religions.

Muslim festivals include the Id-ul-Fitr festival at the end of Ramadan and Mouloud to celebrate Muhammad's birthday. These are times of both feasting and fasting. Christians celebrate at Christmas and Easter.

Hindu stories are celebrated by the *barong* dances on Bali. The *barong* is a creature that brings good luck. He fights and defeats an evil witch called Rangda. In other Balinese festivals, fruit is offered to the gods to celebrate a good harvest.

A woman on Bali dancing the traditional barong dance.
- *The dance has slow and graceful movements.*
- *This is a colourful event that tourists come to enjoy.*

Local festivals

Festivals are held to celebrate the ancient kings in different parts of Indonesia. One such festival is at Surakarta on Java where two royal families lived.

Women on Bali carrying gifts to a Hindu temple.
- *There are about 30,000 temples on Bali.*
- *On Bali, people combine Hindu, Buddhist and other beliefs.*

Some traditions are local to their own small areas. On the island of Flores, the Caci festival is traditional at weddings. First, the parents of the bride and groom agree on a price for the bride. Next a pig's liver is studied to see what the future will bring. Then the village men attack each other with whips made from buffalo hide. They do this to show how brave they are in front of the village women. Many of the men are badly cut and bruised, but it is only done in fun.

Some traditional ceremonies are now performed just to entertain the tourists. These ceremonies are likely to lose their real meaning as more tourists are encouraged to come to watch.

The Toradjan tribespeople on Sulawesi used to be head-hunters. They have stopped this custom and are now peaceful farmers instead.

Women rule

In the western end of Sumatra, the Minangkabaus women make most of the important decisions. The woman's name is passed on when she marries. Women ask the men to be their husbands. Women own the land and other property. This is a very peaceful part of Indonesia.

There is a national holiday on 17 August to celebrate Indonesia's independence.

29

INDONESIA FACTFILE

Area 1,919,443 square kilometres

Highest point Mount Jaya 5029 m

Climate

	January temp.	July temp.	Total annual rainfall
Jakarta	26°C	27°C	1755 mm

Population 200 million

Population density 110 people per square kilometre

Life expectancy Female 65, Male 61

Capital city Jakarta

Population in towns and cities 33%

Population of the main cities (millions)

Jakarta	8.3
Surabaya	2.4
Bandung	2.0
Medan	1.7
Palembang	1.1
Semarang	1.0

Land use

Forest	60%
Crops	9%
Grass	7%
Other	24%

Employment

Farming	56%
Services	30%
Industry	14%

Main imports
Machinery and electrical equipment
Chemicals
Vehicles
Fuels
Raw materials

Main exports
Crude oil and natural gas
Plywood
Textiles
Rubber
Tea and coffee

Language

Javanese	42%
Sundanese	15%
Malay	6%
Madurese	5%

Note: The official national language is Bahasa Indonesian.

Religions

Muslim	87%
Christian	10%
Hindu	2%
Buddhist	1%

Money
The rupiah

Wealth $US740
Note: This is calculated as the total value of what is produced by the country in one year, divided by its population and converted into US dollars.

GLOSSARY

active (volcano) a volcano that still erupts

archipelago a group of islands

capital city the city where a country has its government

colony a place that is ruled by another country

consumer goods items people buy to use in their homes

coral reefs barriers that are mostly underwater made from both living and dead coral

craft a traditional way of making something

ecotourists tourists who visit an area to enjoy its natural wildlife and vegetation

estates very large farms that are run as businesses

gasfield an area where there is natural gas

habitat an environment for wildlife

independence the right of a country to run its own government

inhabited people live there

kampungs shanty town areas in Indonesian cities

lahars mudflows which run down the slopes of a volcano

logging cutting down trees for timber

mangrove forests a type of forest that grows in coastal areas in the tropics

martial arts ways of defending yourself and training your mind

mass-produced something that is made in large amounts in a factory

monsoon a seasonal change in the main wind direction

multi-national companies companies with branches in many countries

navigable a river that boats can use

paddy fields fields for growing rice

plates very large slabs of the earth's crust

population the people who live in an area

recycled made from materials that have already been used before

shanty town an area of houses that people have built for themselves around the edge of a city, in poor countries

staple foods the main foods that people eat

straits a narrow stretch of water between two areas of land

terraces narrow steps of land cut into a hillside for use as fields

trenches very deep parts of the ocean where plates of the earth's crust meet

tropical rain forest the natural vegetation in very hot and wet tropical areas

tsunami a very large and fast-moving sea wave caused by an underwater earthquake or volcanic eruption

uninhabited nobody lives there

INDEX